IGNITE

20 TOOLS
TO FIRE UP
YOUR LIFE

THE ESSENTIALISTS

I believe it is really important not to just watch life from the sideline. Step forward and give your dreams the very best chance they can to ignite. It's the only way they can possibly come true.

CAROLYN CRESWELL, FOUNDER, CARMAN'S MUESLI

Many people live their lives 'wanting': I want to be thinner, more successful, healthier, fitter, happier, etc., and if you live your life wanting, that is what life will give you, the feeling of wanting. To change your life, you need to ignite those emotions and desires and change them to action. The word ignite means to me getting started. It is the flicker that can create the fire in your life that you desire.

JANINE ALLIS, FOUNDER, BOOST JUICE

To ignite is to find purpose. It's when the embers of a million ideas and past attempts suddenly amass into something tangible and clear.

JOSH JANSSEN & TOMMY JACKETT, THE DAILY TALK SHOW PODCAST

To me, innovation is simply 'change that adds value' –
if you choose to use these twenty *Ignite* tools you will
absolutely fire up and innovate in your life!

JUSTIN BAIRD, INNOVATIONIST

Life is too short not to pursue what lights your
soul on fire. We get so caught up in the glorification
of busy and the achievement conveyer belt,
but what is it all for if it doesn't ignite your passion
and expand your world? The Essentialists bring
these questions to the forefront of our attentions in
an age where we need it most.

SARAH HOLLOWAY, HOST OF SEIZE THE YAY PODCAST

Yet again, The Essentialists have gifted us a
powerful gem in *Ignite*. True to brand, this one is
inspirational, warm and human, yet tactical and
easy to implement. Your body, mind and soul
will eat it up from cover to cover!

BELINDA WALL, FOUNDER, BRAND AMPLIFIED

Contents

PENGUIN BOOKS

UK | USA | Canada | Ireland | Australia
India | New Zealand | South Africa | China

Penguin Books is part of the Penguin Random House group of companies
whose addresses can be found at global.penguinrandomhouse.com.

Penguin
Random House
Australia

First published by Michael Joseph in 2020
This edition published by Penguin Books in 2024

Text copyright © Shannah Kennedy and Lyndall Mitchell 2020

The moral right of the authors has been asserted.

Cover design by Louisa Maggio © Penguin Random House Australia Pty Ltd
Internal design by Louisa Maggio © Penguin Random House Australia Pty Ltd
Typeset by Louisa Maggio © Penguin Random House Australia Pty Ltd

Printed and bound in Australia by Griffin Press, an accredited
ISO AS/NZS 14001 Environmental Management Systems printer

 A catalogue record for this
book is available from the
National Library of Australia

ISBN 978 1 76135 069 6

penguin.com.au

We at Penguin Random House Australia acknowledge that Aboriginal and Torres
Strait Islander peoples are the Traditional Custodians and the first storytellers of
the lands on which we live and work. We honour Aboriginal and Torres Strait
Islander peoples' continuous connection to Country, waters, skies and communities.
We celebrate Aboriginal and Torres Strait Islander stories, traditions and living
cultures; and we pay our respects to Elders past and present.

To our children, Jack, Mia, Poppy and Grace

Believe in your brilliance, honour your talents,
go out into the world and radiate your best.
You are each unique and have the power to live
your dream life. Own your genius.

To our husbands

Thank you for standing beside us as we
continue our quest to journey down the
pathway of personal mastery.

To the reader

May this ignite the fire within you.

INTRODUCTION

Ignite is a collection of personal transformational strategies to spark you into action to expand and optimise your life. This handbook is your essential 'go-to' resource when you are ready to raise the bar, energise your life and upgrade your game. It provides powerful, vital, practical skills for everyone on the planet who wants fresh inspiration. Using these skills as your guide to igniting your quest for personal life mastery will have a major effect on your motivation and, ultimately, your success and happiness.

While simple on the surface, the skills we share here can have a big impact and can be game-changing once you have the courage to act on them and make them a part of your daily practice. It is time to live with eyes wide open, to feel vibrant, inspired, happy and in control of your journey by focusing on strategies that will allow you to break through to the next level.

Ignite will leave you wildly awake with inspiration and passion to evolve and flourish in life.

Shannah and Lyndall – *The Essentialists*

Habits

We first make
our habits,
then our habits
make us.

———

ANONYMOUS

MASTER YOUR HABITS

Habits are those amazing sparks that light your fire and keep it going. Habits build your life, your empire and your depth of happiness, and are responsible for your success. They are the secret to advancing yourself, to fuelling a life you love and cherish. The key is to consistently practise the right habits every single day. There has never been as true a saying as 'Change your habits, change your life.'

Habits are thoughts and behaviours so strongly wired into your mind that you perform them without thinking. They are learned and repeated over time, performed automatically, and are persistent, making them hard to break or change. Most of the day you probably think you are making decisions. However, around 40 per cent of the time, you will just do what you have done before – that is, acting according to your habits. This can make you less productive and less effective than you could be.

Successful people form habits that feed success rather than failure. They do what it takes to get the job done. They own their habits, work with them, master them and consistently review them. Supercharged habits are simple, productive actions, repeated consistently over time, that will fuel your fire. The fire extinguishers are the other habits, simple errors in judgement repeated consistently over time. The choice is simple and it is yours to make every hour, every day.

All our life, so far as it has definite form, is but a mass of habits – practical, emotional, and intellectual – systematically organised for our weal or woe, and bearing us irresistibly toward our destiny, whatever the latter may be.

WILLIAM JAMES

To upgrade and master your habits, identify what is and is not working for you, set up your systems, shift your mindset and find some accountability. Almost everything you do now you could do better. Remember, what you do matters not only for you but for those around you. Your loved ones, friends and co-workers feel the ripple effect of the magnificent or mundane version of yourself you bring to your day-to-day life. Habits need constant attention and fine-tuning, and can be our best friend or our foe.

Greatness is always possible in your moment of decision. The power lies in your simple actions, done consistently, which have a compounding effect and can result in either self-mastery or living a limited existence.

TIPS TO MASTER YOUR HABITS

IDENTIFY YOUR SMALL, LIMITING HABITS – Where in life are you not getting the results you want? Do you want more energy, a healthier, stronger, leaner body, more inner harmony, a clearer mind and some space in life? What do you do daily that is not contributing to allowing this to flourish? Where do you sabotage yourself? Are you too critical of yourself, rather than looking for what you do well and acknowledging it? Do you buy lunch daily, which undermines your savings plan? Turn to sugar rather than moving your body for energy? Waste two hours on social media and distraction each day instead of reading a chapter of a book to upskill yourself? Identify these old habits and swap them over for new ones.

CHECK YOUR INTERNAL LANGUAGE – 'I must have a coffee to start the day.' Actually, you don't. Check where you always say you 'need' and 'must have' something, and question it. Change the computer program in your mind.

What would be an alternative choice that might give you a better result? Instead of coffee, try lemon and water. Instead of 'I must check my emails first thing in the morning', you could journal, meditate, exercise and eat well before you check your email in order to own your morning and look after the greatest asset you have – yourself.

UPGRADE YOUR MINDSET – A mindset is the mental framework with which you approach your daily life. Change your mindset to be expansive and welcoming to the life you really want, rather than falling back on comforts that in fact sabotage your results. Your routine is the manifestation of a habit. We cannot get rid of or extinguish old habits but we can work with them, change them and upgrade them in order to catapult ourselves to stunning success. Focus on what you will gain from the shift of the habit, rather than what you will lose.

START WITH THE 1% – Do you think you could improve yourself – your health, your happiness, your knowledge, your skills, your diet, your relationships, whatever area of life you want to look at – with just 1 per cent of change per day? Challenge yourself daily with 1 per cent improvements for the rest of your life. Start swapping the negative with a positive. Start refining what you do. Start an incredible awareness campaign in your mind about what you actually do with the minutes of your precious days, how those activities make you feel and if they get you the results you actually want.

Routine, in an intelligent man, is a sign of ambition.

———

W.H. AUDEN

All the positive psychology research and writing tells us that you can reprogram your brain through some very simple exercises. It doesn't require any kind of huge, massive effort or difficult personal transformation, nor some breakthrough, nor anything dramatic or heroic or titanic – just fairly mundane, repetitive tasks that are easy to do, and to do again.

Stephen Covey was an American educator, author and businessman. He wrote a bestselling book called *The 7 Habits of Highly Effective People*, which is a guide to developing personal effectiveness, being proactive and taking responsibility for your choices. The seven habits he identified are:

1. **BE PROACTIVE**
This means you are the force behind your personal vision.

2. **BEGIN WITH THE END IN MIND**
Control your own destiny with personal leadership – envision what you want in the future so you can work and plan towards it.

3. **PUT FIRST THINGS FIRST**
Do the hardest thing in your day first.

4. THINK WIN-WIN

Hone your interpersonal leadership.
Understand what motivates others and
work cooperatively with them.

5. SEEK FIRST TO UNDERSTAND, THEN TO BE UNDERSTOOD

There's a reason you have two ears and only
one mouth!

6. SYNERGISE

Focus on creative cooperation with teamwork,
open-mindedness, and the adventure of
finding new solutions to old problems.

7. SHARPEN THE SAW

Focus on principles of balance and self-
renewal. Practise improving the physical,
emotional, mental and spiritual areas
of your life.

Old habits never die, but rather get masked by new ones.
So make the journey enjoyable and something you look
forward to as a challenge, which will make it quicker
and easier. As American philosopher Will Durant once
said, 'We are what we repeatedly do. Excellence, then, is
not an act, but a habit.'

And, remember, you are the average of the five people you surround yourself with most often. Check out the habits of those around you and spend more time around the people who embody the traits you want to create in yourself.

Whether you like it or not, your habits are the magical ingredients for your masterpiece called life. Own them, work with them, fine-tune them and build them into your existence to keep adapting yourself to align with your dreams, visions and goals. Your habits are the only things standing between you and the success you want in your incredible and precious life.

Stress

Stress is the trash of modern life. We all generate it but if you don't dispose of it properly, it will pile up and overtake your life.

———

TERRI GUILLEMETS

TRANSFORM YOUR STRESS

Stress is an integral part of life. The stress response is the body's way of protecting you from threats. Life wants you to win, and when you understand and work with stress you can transform your life, reclaim your energy, vitality and focus, and amplify your resilience. What counts is how you handle your stress. It is time to tame it and turn it to your advantage so you can live a more peaceful and meaningful life.

Many people say they are stressed and suffering from burnout without thinking to pause and evaluate any emotional, mental or physical reactions that are occurring at the time. If you are feeling exhausted, stuck in a rut, at a crossroads or paralysed by the world and feelings of stress, it is time to take back the reins, kickstart yourself, regain control and find solutions to get your flow back.

Stress can be caused by external events, such as sickness, the death of a loved one, a late plane, a traffic jam, changing financial markets, an overwhelming boss, or a lack of clarity on what to do next. However, a large portion of our stress is self-inflicted by our limiting beliefs, our focus on what we cannot control and our lack of commitment to refuelling ourselves. One of our wonderful mentors, Dr James Rouse, always challenges us to find a proactive strategy or mindset shift to move from stressed to blessed.

The key to igniting personal change and banishing energy-zapping, everyday stress is to become an awareness expert. This is a commitment to uncover and change the repetitive patterns in which you find yourself that cause you stress, and engage in more supportive practices. Own your thoughts, your words and your reactions. You have all the tools you need: mindset, ambition, beliefs and free will. If you use them well and become the controller of them, you can optimise your outcomes, live a more balanced life and find personal freedom.

Do you ever find yourself feeling stressed because you have so much on? Exhausted because you haven't had enough sleep? Most likely it is because you dropped the ball on protecting yourself – you said yes to please someone else at the cost of your energy, time and emotion, when it wasn't even a special event. Or you watched another two episodes of a TV show instead of getting to bed and prioritising sleep so you would wake up feeling fresh and inspired. Stress build-up occurs when you fail to take the time to refuel and commit to practices that support your overall general health and wellbeing. To cope well with stress we need perspective, and to have good perspective we need a full fuel tank. Everything is more stressful when you are exhausted.

When you commit to your fundamentals, guard them and upgrade the balance in your life, you will experience a new sense of owning your stress level rather than suffering from it. Once you assume control with effective stress-relief rituals, you will find yourself more emotionally stable, mentally sharp and productive, and you will have world-class energy levels. It is the way you respond to stress, which is a choice you can own, that will have the most profound effect on your mental, physical, emotional and spiritual life.

IDENTIFY HOW YOU WANT TO FEEL – Being calm, confident and fuelled with energy requires you to make great choices. Every day you have multiple opportunities to make choices to support this version of yourself. Commit to putting yourself first, to practising the art of extreme self-care for optimal living, joy, happiness and health. Your habits need to support this vision of yourself.

PRIORITISE YOUR REFUEL – Rise early and move swiftly. Get to bed early and embrace gratitude. Raise the bar with the most basic of human needs: the rest and sleep your body needs to repair itself, to restore, to be able to tackle stress with gusto. Commit to the downtime your body and mind need in order to feel alive with awe and fuelled for take-off each day. Plan your time.

CHALLENGE YOUR MINDSET – A delayed flight is a potential cause of stress, but instead of letting it negatively change the course of your day, ask yourself, 'What is the opportunity?' This unexpected unscheduled time could be a chance to get ahead on some work, listen to a meditation or read a book. If you are stuck in traffic, you could listen to a podcast, enjoy some silence or put on relaxing music to improve your mood. You cannot change the traffic, but you can change how you experience it. A project such as writing a book can be viewed as hard, overwhelming and laborious, or creative, challenging and a chance to grow and extend yourself as a human being. What you tell yourself about a situation will be delivered and expressed through your body, and will often dictate how you feel. Tell yourself you feel terrific, that you are the driver and that you love who you are to grow this muscle of confidence and care for yourself.

HAVE A RESPONSE PLAN – This means mastering the gracious art of saying no and setting your boundaries. When an energy-zapping friend calls for another coffee catch-up, be ready to politely decline. You don't have to go to casual last-minute office drinks if what you would really rather do is get up at 5.30 am the next day to exercise and then deliver a great presentation first thing. By going straight home you can recover from the day, spend some time with a pet or a loved one, take a bath and get some sleep. If you go for drinks you might be tempted by others to stay later, sabotaging all your good intentions. The fear of missing out represents a lack of commitment to wanting to be the best version of yourself.

By focusing on what you can control, which ignites your personal power, you have a chance to tackle the root causes of your stress with energy and a clear mind, and to create action to move forward and find opportunities to be the version of yourself you want to be.

Get out of your own way and transform your stress; get close to it, understand it and work on protecting yourself with strong strategies. Stress will always be present, so harness your ultimate life by mastering your focus on what you can control, and committing to a management plan for easier living.

Health

If you have health, you probably will be happy, and if you have health and happiness, you have all the wealth you need, even if it is not all you want.

ELBERT HUBBARD

SUPERCHARGE YOUR HEALTH

Choosing to invest in your health is one of the most empowering and rewarding decisions you can make every day of your life. It will radically transform the levels of vitality and happiness that you experience on a daily basis. Supercharging your health is boosting your health in every dimension of your life – physically, mentally, emotionally and spiritually. Each of these dimensions act and interact in ways that dramatically impact your quality of life. When you are mentally and physically stronger, you are more naturally optimistic, motivated, resourceful and tenacious. You have more self-confidence and inner strength to deal with whatever life throws your way.

Investing means devoting more time and energy for the purpose of achieving higher levels of health. You only get out what you put in. It is having the drive and desire to continually evolve, grow and reach new heights of physical health that you never thought possible. Your dreams will not eventuate unless you take action. Superb health with great stamina, energy, fire and harmony is the foundation of your brilliant self: the concrete formula on which you can build an awe-inspiring life, live your dreams and experience inner harmony. It is the culmination of daily practices that support your mental, physical, emotional and spiritual health, which will in turn support stunning success.

A high-performing human being is operating at excellence in all dimensions of their life. Making a personal pledge to a life mastery mindset is to commit to continual evolution and desire to be the better version of yourself. Whenever you have the opportunity, choose to upgrade and invest in the most precious, one and only asset that is yourself.

You have choices every day that affect your health, energy and vitality. To live a long and happy life where you optimise your lifestyle, your health needs to become a priority right now. Every choice you make has a distinct impact on your future. The good news is that making choices for your health to thrive does not require a complex grand plan. It all starts with the next choice you make.

TOP TIPS TO RAISE THE BAR ON YOUR HEALTH

PHYSICAL – Challenge and fine-tune how you eat, move and sleep to improve your levels of energy and vitality, as well as your decision-making. Small changes can have big impacts.

Eating – Your body needs high-quality fuel to be in peak condition. Most of us know when we're not making the best choice about the fuel we put into our body. Each week, try to improve what you eat by 5 per cent. Take the time every Sunday to see where you can improve the ROI – return on ingestion – on everything that you put in your body. Choose local, seasonal wholefoods where possible to give you long-lasting, slow-burning fuel rather than a sugar high, crash-and-burn type energy source. Aim for your plate to be composed of half energy-boosting fruit and vegetables, one quarter protein and one quarter carbohydrates. Eating protein-rich foods will replenish your protein stores to help keep stress and cortisol levels low.

Moving – Do whatever it takes to maintain your physical health. Exercise is a fantastic way to release stress, balance your moods and enhance your energy. There is lots of research to show that physical fitness and wellbeing have a direct impact on the strength and flexibility of your mind. Exercise lets valuable endorphins kick in to lift your mood and, in turn, make you feel more positive and self-confident. Find a form of physical activity you genuinely enjoy and do it regularly. Hire a trainer, join a dance club or find a friend to exercise with. Rise early and move your body. A twenty-minute workout can improve your mood for several hours after you finish exercising. Take the stairs where you can and walk to meetings. Even better, book in time to exercise as if it were a meeting and commit to your appointment. Any exercise is better than a day with no vigorous activity at all. Clear thinking and optimism become much easier when you're active and fit.

Sleep – Getting a good night's sleep is like a wash cycle for your brain. It clears your stressors from the day before. Optimise your sleep routine so you can consistently get eight to nine hours per night. Say no to other activities when you need to make your sleep a priority. Sleep is our fuel for better performance and unlocking our full potential. Get to bed by 10 pm, remove technology from your bedroom and make the temperature slightly cooler than usual room temperature to improve the quality of your sleep.

MENTAL – Maintain your mental health by avoiding excessive stress, worry, anxiety and burnout. Find your own personal balance. Leaders see opportunities more than they see obstacles. Upgrading your mental health means continually refocusing your mindset to be more growth-focused, rather than having a fixed mindset. To develop a growth mindset, we must train ourselves to develop an appetite for learning. Those with a growth mindset understand that effort and persistence are the keys to unlocking high mental performance. Start with deleting 'should' and 'can't' from your vocabulary. Meditating regularly can also help to build the muscle of attention and unlock your creative, growth-focused mindset. Read personal development books and attend workshops and conferences to extend your knowledge.

EMOTIONAL – The way we process our emotions is central to how they affect you. Walk away from people or situations that drain you emotionally. Positive emotions, thoughts and feelings will have a knock-on effect and will help bring positive results. For example, being kind to someone in a stressful situation, such as when you are exchanging insurance details after a minor car accident, will yield much better results than a negative approach. When we can allow, feel, control and regulate our reactions to our emotions we can reach higher states of emotional equilibrium and, ultimately, happiness. Practices to develop and master your emotional intelligence are journalling, mindfulness and breathing exercises.

SPIRITUAL – Maintain your spiritual health by finding meaning in the things you do. Whatever has meaning for you is the spiritual leader in your life that aligns you with a life of mastery and greater purpose. Upgrading your internal and external faith every day is stepping closer to the path of being an adaptable student of life. Listen more to your internal messages; view your intuition as a valuable data source that you need to stop and listen to. When you're grounded and feeling strongly connected with your core, your intuition or 'gut feeling' on things becomes much clearer. When you learn how to respond to what it is telling you, your certainty around decision-making and life in general increases.

When you take full ownership for your life and the choices you make, it is one of the most empowering and freeing commitments you will ever make. To do so, you must be aware of the choices you make every single day. When you become more mindful of what you think and how you navigate life, you start to enjoy optimum levels of health in all its dimensions. This focus is increasingly essential for thriving and succeeding in a world full of distraction, where people seek temporary entertainment over long-term enrichment. It's about turning down the noise and becoming more focused on what's within. When you do so, you're able to access and harness your creativity, your authenticity, your mission and your highest, most brilliant potential.

Take responsibility, step up and don't settle for middle-of-the-road health. Reach further and achieve peak performance physically, mentally, emotionally and spiritually, and you will be unstoppable.

Money

More important than the how we achieve financial freedom, is the why. Find your reasons why you want to be free and wealthy.

___

ROBERT KIYOSAKI

CREATE FREEDOM OF CHOICE

Money might not buy happiness, but it is hard to be happy if you cannot meet your basic needs. Freedom of choice comes from financial wellbeing: in other words, how effectively you manage your economic life. When you upgrade your financial habits you can eliminate unnecessary stress caused by debt and lack of control, and give yourself the space to grow, evolve, flourish and live life with vitality.

Creating world-class financial wellbeing is about how you manage your personal finances and where you put this discipline on your priority list. Often it is not about how much money you make but rather how and where you are spending it. People with strong financial wellbeing manage their finances well, value experiences over material possessions, and have the capacity and mindset to want to give to others. They have the opportunity to live life with passion and excitement as a result of taking full responsibility for their finances.

Having a plan for your money gives you peace of mind. It gives you calm and confidence, and having a plan for your money can transform your life. You do not need to be a millionaire to feel or be successful. You have the opportunity to feel successful by having some great financial goals with simple and clear plans in place to support them. By failing to take into account what you want for your future self, you risk entering mid-to-late life without the savings you will need to have the choices you will want. Saving or investing some of your current income is an essential part of your financial success, along with not falling into the temptation of the buy-now, pay-later mentality that comes with access to credit.

KNOW YOUR GOALS – Clarity is key. What do you want to create for your future self? What brings you joy that you need money for? Is it an annual holiday, a car, to own your home, to be debt free, or to indulge in a passionate hobby that will require further education? Know what you want to save for and get emotionally attached to, what you will gain by having such goals and the joy you will have when you get there.

PLAN YOUR MONTH AHEAD – If you have everything you need, avoid going to sales with friends for the sake of it. Don't put yourself in a position of temptation if it is not part of your goals. Plan where you can trim your spend. Do you really need two TV streaming services, as well as cable TV? Do you really need to go to every lunch you are invited to, or buy your lunch every day when you could make it and bring to work? Where can you fine-tune your month ahead and the spend involved?

CHECK YOUR MONEY – Designate one day of every month as 'finance day': a day to check in with your money and take note of what came into the accounts and what went out during the previous month. Hone your knowledge, gain clarity and become friends with your bank accounts and the flow of those valuable fun vouchers called money. When your spreadsheets are done once every month, you can see the factual evidence of what actually happened over the previous month.

SET CHALLENGES – Upskill yourself and challenge yourself to treat your finances like an exciting new puppy: something that needs training, brings you joy and will reward you for your efforts. Change your mindset around money. You should think of it as something that is exciting and liberating, and that you will work with for the remainder of your life, in a wonderful journey of growth and abundance.

CHECK YOUR CONSUMPTION

You probably don't need to make more money, and for most of us that is to some degree out of our control anyway. What is in your control is what you spend. Do you want to keep up with your friends, neighbours or colleagues as they buy new clothes and constantly follow fashion trends, upgrade cars and furnishings, and keep filling gaps in their lives by spending rather than simplifying? Understand that you don't have to follow someone else's definition of success; instead, you can find your own and create uplifting, liberating long-term rules and goals for your life journey. The more you lock in to high levels of consumption during any stage of your life, the harder it is to adapt to lower levels in retirement. People tend to save inadequately for retirement and have fewer choices because saving or investing means postponing or foregoing current consumption to shift money from today to tomorrow.

What small but magnificent steps are you willing to take today to reach your idea of financial freedom?

Planning for the future might mean you need to hold off some short-term delights to allow your long-term goals to come to fruition. Automate your structure to create a strong financial habit and reduce the opportunities for you to self-sabotage. This could mean setting up an automatic transfer into a savings account every pay day, setting up a voluntary superannuation contribution with your employer, or setting up your bills to be automatically deducted from your bank account. Follow this up with your monthly review and updates to remain aware and in control.

Jump in, spark up this part of your life, embrace your money, own it, love it and work with it to create the lifestyle and feeling of freedom that will lead to personal fulfilment in life.

I believe that through knowledge and discipline, financial peace is possible for all of us.

———

DAVE RAMSEY

5

Vision

Vision is a
destination –
a fixed point
to which we focus
all effort.
Strategy is a route –
an adaptable path
to get us where
we want to go.

SIMON SINEK

AMPLIFY YOUR VISION

Vague visions equal vague results. To stay ultra-inspired – to extend yourself, to stretch and embrace your goals with purpose, excitement and courage – dig deeper into your vision, hopes and dreams. Take a little precious time to unlock your brilliance, your pathway and your unapologetic greatness through dreaming big and pledging to live your best life.

If you have found yourself living life well and aligned with your vision, then you may have already successfully implemented that life skill from our previous book, *Shine: 20 secrets to a happy life*. Now it is time to take the next step, to amplify, to take the challenge to sharpen your awareness of what you want so you can make better choices in your daily life. Your personal vision and mission can inspire and shift your motivation into a higher gear, transform your life and change your world. It has been said that if you don't have a plan for your life, you will live by someone else's plan.

Where your focus goes, your energy flows. Those who amplify their vision put fear aside, allow themselves to be limitless, create excitement for their own lives and, most importantly, get emotionally connected with what they hope for. It is time to revisit your vision, to dig deeper, to get clearer and more specific, and bring it all to life.

Your dreams are the highest expression of your inner world. They can be wild and free and show you your brilliance. Your dreams open the doorway for you to create a vision for yourself that excites you, inspires you and lights up your inner drive to make the most of your precious life.

GET YOUR VISION OUT – Gather up your old vision boards, vision statements and records of your old dreams. You may have ticked some off, you may have achieved many of them, or you might find your priorities have shifted. If you are resetting your vision, it is time to stop, to reassess, and to think bigger. Bring out your old visions so you can touch and reconnect with them, then make new statements, put up new pictures, recreate your vision and inject excitement to it.

GET SERIOUSLY CONNECTED – Connect emotionally, physically and spiritually to what you want to create for yourself. Do you really want it? Will you love it? Are you passionate about it? Does it create excitement for you and inspire you to take action? Take the time to ensure the words in your vision are right for you, the pictures sing to you and it sparks feeling and emotion when you look at it.

CREATE MOVEMENT – Prioritise your dreams and goals, and take serious action by looking at your habits and your diary to determine how you spend your time and who you are connecting with to bring these dreams to life. What small commitment can you make to move forward today? Set some smaller, achievable goals to get closer to your vision.

One goal a month equals twelve great steps a year towards achieving your vision. Join a yoga class (and book in the next 10 classes while you are there), enlist a mentor, sign up to the course you always wanted to do, de-clutter your home by choosing one room a month to totally overhaul, get your finances in order one day a month, stock the pantry with the right foods for you, start a book club, and block out time in your diary to work on yourself.

EMBRACE THE DREAM – Your visions, hopes and dreams need to be a part of your daily thoughts. Journal about them, write them out, create some mind maps of them, enlist a support team, a mentor and an accountability partner. This keeps your visions at the top of your mind and ensures they are a priority in your decision-making processes. We keep our visions on the bathroom mirror and on big pin boards in our offices. They are there to inspire us and guide us daily. There is no forgetting about them or escaping them – they are in front of us constantly to be a source of light.

DEVELOP A LIFELONG HABIT – Your vision is to be cultivated forever, to be cared for, to be touched and given serious attention. It will change, evolve and grow as you do. Each year the landscape of your life changes: the environment changes, your family dynamic changes, your body changes, your opportunities open doors and the possibilities change. The key to success is to stay committed to achieving your goals but be flexible in your approach.

Develop some fire in your belly, master your mindset and embrace your vision so you open up opportunities as you look past problems and limiting beliefs. Get contagious, so others around you can fuel your energy as your support team and give you the drive and strength to become unstoppable in firing up the life you want. In doing so you will unleash your incredible power and inner drive, and you will create the life you have always dreamed of.

A dream without a plan is just a wish.

_____

KATHERINE PATERSON

Legacy

We all die.
The goal isn't to
live forever;
the goal is to
create something
that will.

———

CHUCK PALAHNIUK

LEAVE A LEGACY

Thinking about your legacy means deciding upon your own personal vision of how you want to be remembered. It is a motivating force that gives you the opportunity to reflect on what is most important in your life. It helps you to start making your mark on the world today by unlocking your unique potential and pushing yourself to greatness.

What do you want to be known for when you leave this earth? The most influential people, the ones who leave behind incredible legacies, will live on in the hearts of people they touch. Their principles, philosophies, contributions and achievements will spread from generation to generation. But a legacy isn't only something you leave behind after you die.

We all have macro legacies and micro legacies that are dynamically interconnected. Your macro legacies are how you contribute to the universe when you leave, impacted by your change. Your micro legacies are how you contribute to chapters in your life when you leave, impacted by your influence. Every time you move away from a chapter of your life – a workplace, job, school, university, relationship or community – you leave a micro legacy behind you.

Most often people will talk about the legacy you leave behind with your character, behaviour and mindset. It includes how you treated other people, and your actions, and the qualities you brought to life, such as kindness, gratitude, authenticity, inspiration, integrity and care for others.

Imagine your ninetieth birthday party. Everyone who is a part of your life, or who you have influenced in some way, is there. As they get up to toast you on reaching this milestone, what would you like them to say about you? That's what you want your life to stand for. That is a clarifying and motivating place to begin to reflect on your macro and micro legacies, and the impact you want to make in your lifetime.

In *The Top Five Regrets of the Dying*, Bronnie Ware, a palliative care nurse who spent years caring for patients in the final stages of their life, wrote about the five biggest regrets that she saw again and again in her patients. They were:

1. **I WISH** I'd had the courage to live a life true to myself, not the life others expected of me.

2. **I WISH** I hadn't worked so hard.
3. **I WISH** I'd had the courage to express my feelings.
4. **I WISH** I had stayed in touch with my friends.
5. **I WISH** that I had let myself be happier.

Many did not realise until the end that happiness is a choice.

In order to leave a legacy and be remembered for what you want to be remembered for, you need to take action today that contributes to living a life that is without regrets and stays in the hearts of those closest to you for generations to come.

To live a full life at your greatest potential, it is very powerful to reflect on your legacies, or what you want to be known for, often. While it is vital to stay focused on your lifelong vision and moving forward, there is also great value in pulling back from the noise and thinking about how you want to be remembered when you're no longer here. Most commonly, the answer to that question is about contributing to causes and actions that last longer than you will, and how you treat people with your words, actions and behaviours in your everyday life.

Carve your name on hearts, not tombstones. A legacy is etched into the minds of others and the stories they share about you.

SHANNON L. ALDER

Here are some meaningful ways to leave a legacy:

- » **Share your time,** efforts and skills wisely in business, your community or any other activity you perform.
- » **Engage with responsibility,** whether in relationships or on a new journey.
- » **Be curious and open.** Remember that you need to be a student to become a teacher.
- » **Encourage a positive mindset.** You can continually spread an abundance of positive energy.
- » **Create an open door for others.** Lead by example, as friendliness, openness and acceptance can be learned.
- » **Share the spirit of gratitude.** A simple 'please' and 'thank you' wherever you go will help to spread gratitude among others. Appreciation and connection create deeper, more meaningful relationships.
- » **Love what you do and who you do it with.** Be fully present and authentic.
- » **Identify your strengths.** Develop and invest in your skills, and be true to who you are.

- » **Contribute as a role model.** Support causes and people that have meaning and purpose to you.
- » **Be a mentor to others.** Pass down your skills and your know-how.
- » **Write a legacy letter.** This means writing down everything you'd want to tell your loved ones if you knew you didn't have much time to live.
- » **Write your memoir.** You can also record messages for loved ones, or create a photo album or a website dedicated to your legacy.
- » **Right a wrong.** Resentment is like drinking poison and expecting the other person to get sick.

Live your best life by creating a legacy you can be proud of. By taking the first step and practising these simple steps every day, you will find that you will travel a long way in just one year. Life is a choice, and it is yours – live the life you love so that you are leaving a legacy that truly touches your heart and makes a compelling, long-lasting, authentic difference to those around you. Leave a mark, not a blemish.

7

Expertise

Never become so much of an expert that you stop gaining expertise. View life as a continuous learning experience.

— DENIS WAITLEY

BECOME AN EXPERT

To get your genius in action, spark your passion and leap towards your vision, allow yourself to grow and develop on the path to becoming an expert. Developing expertise upgrades your focus, ignites motivation, directs internal energy to your passions and opens the door for your life to find a new richness.

You are already an expert at something. You can be an expert with skills that add to your life, or perhaps you have become an expert at something that doesn't add energy, joy, meaning or purpose. Some people are experts at procrastination, or knowing what is on Netflix for the next month, or pressing snooze on the alarm clock. Success is moving away from the skills that don't add to your life and developing habits in the areas that elevate you to new levels of mastery, to fuel your mighty mission of being a happier, healthier version of yourself.

You don't have to be the best in the world or create a global voice for yourself, but rather simply focus your energy on what you are interested in and develop that to a higher grade. It is deciding to master some skills that will bring you incredible joy, confidence and motivation.

From cooking a dish to perfection, to strategic thinking skills, to leading people, to effectively managing your time, to developing expertise as a coach, arranging flowers proficiently or mastering a musical piece, the opportunities are boundless for us to lift ourselves to a higher level of brilliance. Day to day we are always enlisting the services of people with greater expertise than ourselves. We have a friend who is passionate about growing his own vegetables. He enjoys it, works hard at it as his hobby, and has started to study it. So he is our go-to for when we want to learn more about our growing our own food. Another friend was an accountant and enjoyed taking photos, so she did some online courses, then studied photography and today has a great photography business. She has expertise in this area now that she wants to keep developing and take to the next level. We always have the opportunity to develop our own signature on something we enjoy doing and are passionate about, and can then share it with others.

IGNITING EXPERTISE

CHOOSE AN AREA – What do you want to improve on or develop expertise in? Where will this mastery take you and help you be more successful or happy in life? What do you enjoy doing already that you can work on? For example, if your health is a priority for you, delving into the art of food preparation is key. If mental health is your focus for the long term, committing to meditation is important. If you enjoy a certain type of yoga, study it, practise it daily and immerse yourself in the specifics of it.

BECOME A LIFELONG LEARNER – Part of developing expertise is keeping up with new information that is relevant in your field of study. Continue your education, read books and articles, follow relevant blogs and social media accounts, and attend conferences. For continued motivation, find a mentor, a coach or more experienced individuals to guide your journey, listen to podcasts or seminars from experts in your field, join a learning group and form a community. It has never been easier to accommodate learning in your everyday life.

CONSCIOUS PRACTICE – Expertise takes joyful commitment, invested time and energetic practice. It is not viewed as a chore. Studies have concluded that it takes ten thousand hours to become an expert at something. However, the joy comes when we develop the expertise to take us to a higher level. Practise, practise and practise some more, seek feedback and find a mentor. The commitment is to keep taking your skill to a new level by exploring more, allowing failure, learning more, growing and seeking to do it better. This will take you out of your comfort zone and challenge your views as you discover through the art of practice.

SHARE YOUR EXPERTISE – Teach what you are learning. When you share valuable insights, knowledge and experience, or pass on the methods you have learned, you are allowing your mind to understand it better. When you are teaching, you learn how to express your knowledge clearly and effectively – no matter whether it is social media skills, completing tax returns or breathing techniques to calm the mind, you can improve, grow and upgrade your genius. Write a blog about your learnings or findings, publish some articles, share your thoughts on social media or form a group who wants to learn with you.

Developing expertise is about following what interests you and committing to gaining knowledge, to practising, to understanding and developing a passion, and, finally, sharing it. Choose one interest or choose many – every time you learn and do, you evolve as a human being, add depth to your life and open up the grandeur of 'you'.

Goals

Three decisions that we all control each moment of our lives: what to focus on, what things mean, and what to do in spite of challenges that might appear.

TONY ROBBINS

SET HARD-HITTING GOALS

Hard-hitting goals get results, and will reward you for the fuel and commitment you put into them. They will fast-track your development into a stronger, more confident and more courageous human being. Sharpening your focus and awareness on your values-based goals will inspire you, move you towards your vision and bring energised life and purpose to your day. It is not about doing more to achieve your goals, it is about simplifying and focusing to gain results.

Shining a light on the one or two goals that offer the greatest rewards and mean the most to you brings joy, happiness and a sense of achievement to your life. You can upgrade your life by doing this today. It is incredibly rewarding to set personal life goals and to put in effort, integrity and energy towards reaching them. In your career or business life, it is incredibly satisfying to set challenging goals, to commit and work hard towards them and then bask in the glow of your achievement.

If you have read our book *Shine: 20 secrets to a happy life* then you might have already set SMART goals. SMART provides a framework to improve your chances of succeeding in accomplishing a goal.

To make sure your goals are clear and reachable, each one should be:

- » **S**pecific (simple, sensible, significant).
- » **M**easurable (meaningful, motivating).
- » **A**chievable (agreed, attainable).
- » **R**elevant (reasonable, realistic, results-based).
- » **T**ime-bound (time-based, time/cost-limited, timely).

Having a list of SMART goals is a great starting point, but once you become familiar with them you might need to push yourself a bit further to become passionate about your goals, engaged with and emotionally connected to them, and have them at the front of your mind daily. Successful people have razor-sharp focus on what goals will make the difference, have impact and take them to a new level. To do this, you can transition to HARD goals. HARD goals light up the brain and encourage excellence. A truly effective goal should push and challenge you to achieve great things.

Select one or two goals that are most meaningful to you and apply the HARD goals framework to them: **H**eartfelt, **A**nimated, **R**equired and **D**edicated.

HEARTFELT – Ask yourself why you really want this goal. What will make you passionate about it, want to stick with it and want to give great focus to it? What is the reward you are after, and how will getting it make you feel?

ANIMATED – Describe and discuss how you want your efforts to pan out: tell the story of the goal. What will it do for you in one, three and five years' time? How will it impact your life? Why is it so important?

REQUIRED – What is the time frame? One year, six months, three months, one month, one week? What do you need to do *today* to move it forward, to focus on it? Write down what needs to be accomplished by when. The most powerful approach is working in thirty-day blocks to focus on one month's worth of serious effort at a time.

DEDICATED – What skills do you need? What do you need to learn to make it happen? How will you maintain focus, commitment and drive towards it? Who do you need on your team? How will you be accountable? Outlearn last year's self by acting strongly on your skill base.

By investing in these questions you will reveal crystal-clear reasons why you want to commit to your goal. This should spark up your wholehearted desire to move forward.

The essential elements for any goal to succeed are:

DAILY CONTACT – This fires up your mindset. Do a daily goal review to keep clearing out the clutter, noise and distraction. Daily contact with your goals helps you continually realign your tasks and keeps your mind on track. It should be the base of your planning. Take five minutes a day to read your goals in order to imprint them onto your subconscious mind.

WRITTEN WORDS – Writing is committing. To see it on paper, to unlock your words for high-impact activities, brings further clarity, and what is clear in your mind can then be expressed clearly to others.

ACCOUNTABILITY – Surround yourself with people who support you to achieve your goals and help you with your accountability. Be mindful of the people who count; the people who are important to you along with the people who will be there to inspire you when you need it. Be accountable to yourself as well: do the small things daily. Five little goals completed each day leads to 1825 goals in one year. In order to achieve, do small, do daily and do accountability.

BREATHING – Take breaks to re-energise. The most successful people know how to avoid burnout. Have routines that renew and nourish you that are non-negotiable in place in your daily and weekly schedules. (For some ideas, see our book *Restore: 20 self-care rituals to reclaim your energy*.)

Take a proactive mindset, act daily, sharpen your focus and dismiss the disease to please as hard-hitting goals light up your mind, body and soul, and encourage you to grow and thrive in life. Abundant opportunities will open up to you as you reach new heights by simplifying and committing to your goals.

The only limit to the height of your achievements is the reach of your dreams and your willingness to work hard for them.

MICHELLE OBAMA

9

Grit

No grit,
no pearl.

———

ANONYMOUS

BUILD YOUR GRIT

Grit – your perseverance and passion for long-term goals – is the quality that keeps your goals alive through adversity and plateaus, which are all part of our dreams turning into reality. Angela Duckworth, a professor of psychology at the University of Pennsylvania, has concluded that 'where talent counts once, effort counts twice'.

Have you ever found yourself all fired up with ambitious goals and bubbling with excitement, and you get started with enthusiasm and inspiration, but after a while your motivation wears off and life gets in the way – you get distracted, you start to doubt yourself, you start procrastinating and you are back at the start, discouraged and with a dint in your self-confidence? Developing grit is a pursuit to build mental toughness, strengthening the muscle so that it won't give up so easily when you experience a hardship or bump in the road.

Duckworth's research concluded that soldiers with high grit were most likely to complete demanding military training, and that, when comparing two adults of the same age, it is their grit that more accurately predicts who will be better educated and the better employee. She also found that school-age participants in the National Spelling Bee outperformed their peers not because of higher IQ but greater commitment to consistent practice.

Grit can be developed in order to ignite the power of your goals and dramatically increase the chances of you accomplishing your dreams. Here are some exercises to start strengthening your grit:

1. **DEFINE WHAT MENTAL TOUGHNESS MEANS TO YOU –** Is it exercising every day no matter what the weather is like? Is it writing in your journal for ten minutes a day, even when you don't feel like it? Or is it reading ten pages a day to upskill, and making that practice a non-negotiable for a whole year?

2. **START WITH SMALL BITS OF GRIT –** The grit muscle needs to be exercised all the time, rather than just once a week. Do that extra push-up when you have done your planned ten. Switch your mindset around when doing a boring chore like ironing and turn it into a mindful activity. Pick up the phone in a difficult situation rather than sending a text. Get up when your alarm goes off to fulfil a promise to yourself. Give yourself

only ten minutes, twice a day, to check your social media.

3. **BUILD BULLETPROOF HABITS** – Rely on habits, which are second nature, rather than relying on motivation, which can be affected by so many external factors. Build habits that support your goal, which will offer you a solution when inspiration is lacking, because they are ingrained. People with grit are consistent: they stick to their schedules, they have great plans and solid systems. They don't rely solely on courage, talent, skill, intelligence or motivation, but they are stunningly successful with consistency. If you want to exercise every morning you need to make it habitual: book it in as a meeting, set the alarm every night, put your exercise clothes next to the bed and honour your promise to yourself.

Grit-based leaders are there for their staff, they have clear goals, they manage their time strictly, and they don't let a bad result or unsuccessful meeting derail them from their mighty vision. They work to a schedule, even when they don't feel like it; they approach their work with a positive, professional mindset, do the most important things first and take responsibility.

Angela Duckworth makes the following recommendations about how to build the muscle of grit into your life.

» **Pursue what interests you**
When you commit to doing things that interest you, grit is much easier to build.

» **Practise, practise, practise**
Undertake deliberate practice with the aim to upskill. Our motivation builds as we get better at doing something.

» **Find purpose**
Find your 'why'. Connect to a higher purpose and let it be your inspiration on a daily basis.

» **Have hope**
This means finding your growth mindset, empowering yourself and using language that is positive to cultivate hope and amplify your success.

» **Join a gritty group**
You are who you hang out with. Surround yourself with people with grit that inspire you. Their beliefs, feelings and behaviours will be contagious.

Grit is the driver of your success and your achievement, independent of your intelligence and talents. To thrive in life, to upgrade your game, to transport yourself to a whole new level of inspiration, you need to be able to persist and not throw in the towel so quickly. It is only with effort that talent can lead to success. Grit will always trump talent, so put this in your toolkit of powerful daily practices for success. The person who perseveres is surely the one who will win.

To be gritty is to
keep putting one
foot in front of the other.
To be gritty is to hold
fast to an interesting
and purposeful goal.
To be gritty is to invest,
day after week after year,
in a challenging practice.
To be gritty is to fall
down seven times,
and rise eight.

———

ANGELA DUCKWORTH

10

Wisdom

It is by logic
that we prove,
but by intuition
that we discover.

HENRI POINCARÉ

DISCOVER YOUR WISDOM

Connecting to your wisdom means turning up the volume on your inner voice and following the profound, authentic knowledge already within you. Your wisdom is a calming, non-judgemental force; it is your secret weapon for success. It speaks the language of feelings and senses rather than words and numbers. Connecting to your inner wisdom is owning your genius. As little kids we all listened to our inner voice; however, as we grow older, many of us forget how to access this transformational, powerful life tool.

A mind that is attuned to your inner wisdom will become more efficient at fulfilling your deepest, most authentic desires. Without this inner guidance your mind can easily get distracted and start pursuing other people's desires and needs, like your friends', your parents', your peer group's, or even those that are communicated through advertising. Over time this can create resentment and frustration, when you choose to do what you are 'supposed to' instead of what your intuition is guiding you to do.

It is easy to get into the habit of searching, seeking and rushing from one thing to the next to keep ourselves distracted from uncomfortable feelings. Stop running away from yourself and, instead, run towards yourself.

We are all influenced by life happening around us. It is natural and healthy to have a desire to check in and see where we sit with the rest of the world. Problems start when you listen too much to outside sources and disregard your own inner voice. Then you begin living out of alignment with your values and who you really are. How often do you avoid listening to your intuition? Do you allow the noise from the outside world to over-shadow your wisdom and the truth living within you?

Your inner wisdom is a subtle, gentle whisper of truth. In your decision-making process you have the choice of trusting your logical mind or your intuition. We tend to believe that logical thinking is our main way of thinking and that intuition is a much lower, secondary priority, when in fact all moments of insight and inspiration are the result of intuitive thinking. Think back to your last light-bulb moment – that is an example of your intuition in all its glory.

A recent Australian documentary film called *PGS: Intuition Is Your Personal Guidance System* documents Bill Bennett's quest to understand intuition after a near-death experience in which a mysterious voice saved his life. After years of research with some of the world's leading experts on intuition, spanning the fields of science, religion and spirituality, Bennett concluded that intuition is a part of a subtle energy system that seeks to protect us and guide us along our life's journey so that we can achieve our true purpose. He says, 'It is the first voice that you hear, it is the one that comes to you loud and clear.' The question is, are you ready to follow that voice and trust your own powerful intuition?

We are so familiar with trusting the facts that accessing our inner wisdom can be a challenge. Successful people know when to use different tools and skills and when to follow their intuition. Beginning the process of accessing your own wisdom is a balance of asking these two questions with equal weight:

> » **What do the facts tell me?**
> » **What do I feel?**

There are daily practices of reconnection that can take us closer to our inner wisdom. The most powerful way of being able to listen to your intuition is to be silent. In silence you allow for your own wisdom to come to the fore. Let all the distracting thoughts settle and find the answer you are looking for. It can sometimes take time for the inner-wisdom data download from the cloud of collective consciousness to happen. Come home to your-self and trust that you have the answers. When you feel at home with yourself you begin to feel safe in the world and you start to listen and pay attention to your intuition.

5 WAYS TO PRACTISE LISTENING TO YOUR INNER WISDOM

1. **AWARENESS** – As you go through your day, simply notice the messages and signals your intuition sends you. Be aware of them rather than blocking them out. Awareness is the first step in shifting to a higher level of inner wisdom.

2. **SPACE** – When you have free time, don't rush to the to-do list that could otherwise rule every waking hour. Sit quietly and ask your body, 'What should I do now?' The answer might be something you need but never give yourself. Reduce the environmental noise around you so you have the mental space to listen. Sometimes this might reveal some uncomfortable feelings; use your strength of perseverance to sit with the feelings so you can process them in a healthy way.

3. **PRACTISE** – To get your muscle of intuition fit, lean and healthy, we need to work it regularly. A daily practice of meditation will create the life-transforming habit of connecting to your inner wisdom more often. Your mind is like a garden – weed out the plants you don't want and grow those you prefer.

4. **ACTION** – Once you have learned to listen to your inner wisdom, make sure you apply it to the world around you. Have the confidence to take action on what is right for you. Live life from the inside out, not the outside in.

5. **TRUST** – We are all a work in progress. It takes patience, practice and willingness to discover your inner self, but once you awaken and connect with your wisdom, anything is possible.

6. **SURROUND** – Spend as much time as possible with people who lead by example and also follow their intuition. It is refreshing, motivating and inspiring for you, and good for the planet.

Often you have to rely on intuition.

BILL GATES

11

Productivity

Knowing others
is intelligence,
knowing yourself
is true wisdom.
Mastering others
is strength,
mastering yourself
is true power.

LAO TZU

WORLD-CLASS PRODUCTIVITY

Productivity amplifies life and heightens your success like no other skill. Being productive is about turning up the dial on your pace so you rise above procrastination and fast-track yourself to flourishing, cultivating growth and mastering your personal potential with confidence and energy.

Make the journey to your goals clear and ultra-inspiring, and accomplish your mighty missions with joy. Productivity describes the efficiency with which you execute the tasks that bring your dreams to fruition, and how swiftly you can get through your to-do list in your quest for the rewards you are seeking. You could say it measures your output per unit of input. You want maximum results for the minimum amount of input.

Do you ever wonder how you will get there; how others get so much done as they rise through the ranks? The answer is that they are masters of productivity. They keep upgrading their game of life by setting simple intentions and owning their time and energy. They are constantly taking control to grow and beat pesky distractions and procrastination, which kill the quality of your output and slow the pace of your journey to personal mastery.

Lives are noisy, minds overstimulated and the world complex, leaving many stuck in the distraction and procrastination space. Unable to gain traction on dreams, ideas and goals, you can find yourself looking at others and feeling left behind as they surge ahead at a great rate with fearlessness and energy. They have purity of focus. They are fuelled by clarity and meaningful missions. They have risen above the distraction and procrastination, changed their story, taken control of their mindsets and formed new habits that support productivity and growth.

By upgrading your productivity skill set you will soar, you will create energy, freedom and space, and you will fast-track the journey to where you want to get to. Raise the bar for yourself, boost your confidence and transform your results by introducing these simple and effective game-changing habits to support the powerful tool of productivity. It is exciting to take control, to inject energy into your projects and to amplify your results by embracing this transformative, proven technique and tap into your brilliance.

Productivity occurs when you break down your dreams, goals and aspirations into achievable tasks. Inspiration then springs to life with clarity, as you organise tasks, commit to and engage with them, and simply just *do* them without a story. Your stories create procrastination – excuses as to why you will not be good at it, you may not be enough, know enough, or be qualified enough. Learn and do, and don't allow excuses to come in and rob you of the results you desire. Productivity also occurs when you get rid of the noise and distractions, and find the discipline to just do.

Productivity is simple. It is a powerful path to personal growth and change.

HOW TO MASTER THE
ART OF PRODUCTIVITY

OWN YOUR LIST – Every Sunday, plan your week. Your brain needs a map for the week ahead. Identify the non-negotiables for the week, cultivate the process in your mind for you to soar and create your lifestyle of optimism, because you are the driver. Write down your list – the brain finds incredible motivation from seeing the written word.

MOVE YOUR BODY – Load up your energy tank by getting up early every single day and moving, to fire up your mind, body and soul. Move, unlock and get the flow of life going.

EAT THE FROG – Do the hardest thing in the day first. Get the most challenging tasks, or the most boring ones, out of the way first.

TURN OFF – When getting into a task, disconnect from your devices so you can just focus, do it, tap into your personal power and become profitable with your time. Turn everything off, focus and tick off the task.

HYDRATE – Beat lethargy by drinking a litre of water before you start working, and a litre in the second part of the day. The majority of people are dehydrated and lethargic, therefore lacking the fuel to fire up their motivation.

10-MINUTE POWER JOLTS – Give yourself two ten-minute power jolts per day to reset your intention for the next few hours. You can do this by writing down what you need to achieve in the next three-hour block so you are clear about what needs to be done and ready to dive in. Reset your map with intentions and energy, and leave the cult of average behind.

BRING IN BOUNDARIES – Protect your day, protect yourself and protect your results by setting boundaries. This could mean stand-up meetings, walking meetings, making an agenda and setting a time limit for meetings, not having a coffee until you have ticked off one-third of your to-do list. Put up the boundary fence so time- and energy-robbers have difficulty infiltrating your space.

IDENTIFY YOUR REWARDS – Know what your reward is for the focus and energy you are putting in. For example, if you practise speaking in a language you are learning for 30 minutes, the reward might be to watch 30 minutes of television. If you prepare your food for the day, the reward is that you get to buy a coffee at lunchtime. If you read for 30 minutes something that aids you in your quest to grow and learn, the reward could be to indulge in your social media for 20 minutes, with a time limit on it.

Set intentions to really hack your procrastination and rock your productivity. The aim of productivity is to achieve your results with flair and brilliance by being committed, clear and fully engaged with how you are spending your time.

Develop a winning mindset, know what you want to stop doing and what you want to start, own your time, focus on what matters and use technology appropriately. Build a toolbox of productivity skills so that you can move through life with more ease, greater results, and flourishing, calm confidence.

12

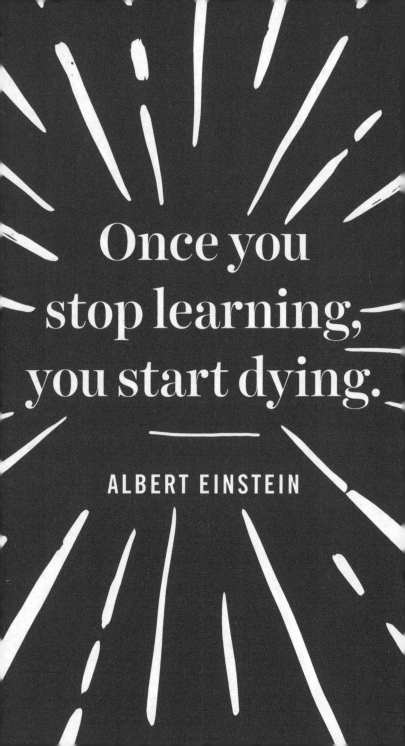

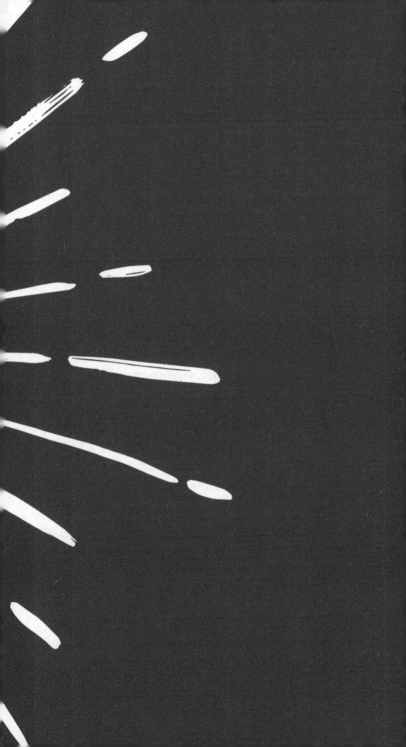

BE A STUDENT OF LIFE

Learning new things is in itself a form of growth and success – a process of igniting, expanding and deepening your knowledge and wisdom. When you choose to be a student of life, you open up yourself to limitless life opportunities. As human beings, we have a natural desire to learn and progress.

Whatever your personal or professional goals are, making a commitment to lifelong learning is a key ingredient for success. Learning doesn't stop when you finish school or university. Life offers more lessons than school ever could.

Successful ageing and longevity are built upon patterns of lifelong learning. When you are intensely engaged in doing and learning new things, your wellbeing and happiness can reach greater levels. Like any muscle, your brain requires regular training and exercise to stay at peak performance. Continual learning keeps your mind working and engaged.

Think about what might work for you. For some it is taking up a new hobby, or broadening their skills and knowledge in an area that has purpose and meaning to them. For us, taking up golf lessons is a way of developing a skill that we can use later in life. Now is not the right time to invest too much time in the skill; however, in our sixties and seventies, having a great technique and knowledge of the game will be a really useful starting point. Every Friday when we are in Melbourne, we get together with five fun and inspiring girlfriends and have a golf lesson. We see this intentional activity as an investment in our future. That is a part of life mastery and contributes to a sense of learning, development and purpose for us.

By having the attitude of being a student of life, you are adopting a growth mindset of continual learning and improvement. Every master thinks like a beginner – they have a deep passion and thirst for learning. Ongoing learning provides you with opportunities to dramatically improve your career, your quality of life and even your health.

Leadership guru Robin Sharma believes that great leaders are devoted readers. One reason he gives is that 'You can spend your evenings, or mornings, or afternoons, or lunchtimes connecting with the greatest minds who have ever graced the planet.' He also says that reading helps to sustain hope and faith. When you read about others people's adversities, and also about solutions to challenges you might face, it gives you a new understanding as well as tools to get past the roadblock and move forward to new heights of success, resilience, focus and motivation.

Every day our minutes matter, and we have choices about how we spend this precious resource. If you want to optimise your minutes and transform them into life-changing insights that heighten your thinking, then make a commitment to continual learning. Remove the autopilot distractions of entertainment that surround you and go further to learn and expand your knowledge.

WAYS TO UNLOCK YOUR STUDENT-OF-LIFE MINDSET

CREATE A COMMUNITY OF LIKE-MINDED PEOPLE – We recently created a learning book club. We gathered a group of inspiring individuals who share a commitment to continual learning and development. Every six weeks we get together to share our insights from our chosen biography, personal-development or leadership book. From these insights we choose one as a takeaway to implement in our lives or our businesses. This book group community creates an energy-boosting dimension of inspiration and vitality in our lives, as well as making us accountable to our goal of continual learning.

LEARNING ON THE GO – Use your downtime to maximise your learning. Transit time is also precious time that could be utilised for learning. When you are driving, on the train, on a plane or in a taxi, make a commitment to listening to an educational, energy-boosting, creative audiobook or podcast. It makes your transit productive and amplifies your learning.

ASK THE QUESTION – To have a curious student of life mindset, ask yourself daily, 'What do I find interesting right now?' Allow the answer to come from your intuition and follow that up with exploration. It may take you on pathways you never dreamed of, and open up unimaginable possibilities.

EXPLORE THE WORLD – If you have the means, go beyond the place you call home. The benefits of getting outside your comfort zone and interacting with other cultures and peoples are immense. It builds confidence and empathy, and strengthens our sense of self, while at the same time helping us to feel connected to others. Have a bucket list of global destinations as well as some local adventures. You will get to experience how a new community or culture lives, works, eats and plays, which will open your mind and remind you of the bigger picture in life. You can adopt this mindset even if you are not physically travelling very far. Be a tourist in your own town, take yourself out of your routine and explore areas and experiences that you wouldn't normally see.

ACQUIRE NEW SKILLS – There are definitely things you don't know how to do, and you have a lifetime ahead of you to learn. It's never too late to start learning something new. Enrol in an online or night class and gain skills in something you consider useful, like learning Spanish for your upcoming trip to Spain, or learning a language that will help you communicate better with people in your life or your community.

TAKE A BEGINNER'S MINDSET – Go deeper to learn more about the food you eat, the exercise you do, the breathing technique you have adopted, your meditation practice or your daily mindset. Constantly remind yourself that, in every area of your life, you can dive deeper and unlock more insight, knowledge and understanding.

DEVELOP YOUR GROWTH MINDSET – One of the core paths towards ongoing learning is cultivating the right mindset. We all have traits of a fixed mindset and a growth mindset. To keep your mindset supple and positive, you can benefit from transforming your fixed-mindset triggers into growth-mindset opportunities. To learn more about maximising your growth mindset, we think the book *Mindset: Changing the way you think to fulfil your potential* by Carol Dweck is a fantastic starting point – if you're like us, you'll want to listen to or read it over and over again! Every time you read or listen to the book you will learn more for different stages of your life.

Live a life
that is driven
more strongly
by curiosity
than by fear.

———

ELIZABETH GILBERT

13

Courage

We must have courage to bet on our ideas, to take the calculated risk, and to act. Everyday living requires courage if life is to be effective and bring happiness.

MAXWELL MALTZ

THE POWER OF COURAGE

The word 'courage' comes from the Old French word *corage*, meaning 'heart'. In this sense, we can think of courage as the ability to stand by your heart or your core. It is living your passion and your purpose out loud and boldly, without exceptions. Courageous people step outside their comfort zones to meet the challenges that lie ahead. Their focus isn't on money or the accumulation of things, but on showing up and living with integrity.

Every act of courage involves accepting a fear. We all face choices that take us out of our comfort zones, and when we decide to take a step forward and discover a new part of ourselves, fear is our trusty companion not far behind. To continually move forward you are saying yes to growing, evolving, transforming and to the power of courage. Whenever you move out of your comfort zone you will naturally feel fear. When you start to accept the inevitability of that fear, its intensity seems to dissipate over time. Courage is not the absence of fear. It is the strength to be who you are in spite of the fear.

What is important is to make your courage bigger than your fears, and to focus your energy on personal shifts that transform your fear into bravery. It is never losing sight of the big picture and the 'why' of what you are doing when you are doing it.

A great place to begin developing your courage is connecting to all the unique and wonderful parts of you – being proud of who you are and what fuels your fire. To be real. Not faking it. This means letting go of others' expectations of you and stopping living life according to other people's desires and needs. An extension of this is knowing who you are and what you stand for. Courageous people know the difference between right and wrong. They don't just talk about integrity, they live it every day, backing their words with action. You always know where courageous people stand. They're passionate about their beliefs and values, and have consistent and predictable behaviour. And though it's not always the easy road, it delivers exponentially higher rewards of happiness and joy.

Start by asking yourself these three powerful questions:

1. What would I do if I wasn't limited by fear?
2. What would I do if I didn't have to be answerable to anyone?
3. Who do I admire as a mentor, and why?

Courage is a skill available to everyone. It is something that we can intentionally cultivate, practise and hone over time to bring us closer to living our happiest, biggest, boldest lives. It adds adventure to our days and brings rich, meaningful culture to the tapestry of our lives.

The seemingly insignificant, everyday actions you implement that take you out of your comfort zone will all add up and build your confidence to do bigger things over time. These small steps will help to develop your confidence and your capacity to do more.

In building strategies for living a more productive, happy and meaningful life, developing courage is yet another way to take responsibility for your state of mind, your circumstances and your wellbeing.

When you recognise your courage, no matter how small and insignificant the situation might be, it is empowering and satisfying. It fuels your confidence and your personal and professional power. If you constantly dismiss how you act with courage instead of pausing to acknowledge it, that keeps you small.

Professional athletes train themselves to manage their emotions and create an aura of invincibility even when they are dealing with high stress and fear. We can learn from this training and adapt these disciplined practices into our daily lives.

5 WAYS TO MAKE FRIENDS WITH FEAR AND EXPAND YOUR COURAGE

1. **FACE FEAR** – It is natural to be fearful of following our hearts or exposing our souls. Ask yourself if you are afraid because you're facing danger or because you might face failure. One is an evolutionary protection mechanism, but the other will hold you back. Fear can be a tool of evolution and growth.

2. **EXPLORE VULNERABILITY** – We project authenticity when we share our experiences of trial and error. When we choose transparency and honesty over perfection, authenticity is unveiled.

3. **TAKE RISKS** – Courageous leaders love the race of their own heartbeat. They are not afraid to take risks, which inevitably develops self-confidence and generates confidence in others. Taking risks helps you to become more authentic, more confident and more courageous.

4. **CELEBRATE DISAPPOINTMENTS** – We become more human and accessible through failure. Using mistakes to your advantage unleashes your potency. Recognise the hidden gift of renewal failure offers – the permission to begin again, and again.

5. **TAKE ACTION** – The challenge is to use fear as a guidepost of where to move to next; to know when to take action even when it isn't always the safe, popular option is an act of courage.

The brave man is not he who does not feel afraid, but he who conquers that fear.

NELSON MANDELA

14

Comfort zone

Life begins at the end of your comfort zone.

NEALE DONALD WALSCH

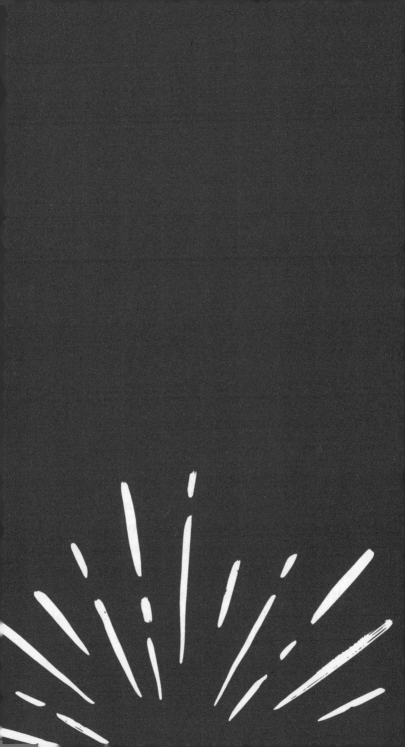

CHALLENGE YOUR COMFORT ZONE

Taking a step into the unfamiliar is living life wide awake, and challenging the day to day by continually supercharging your life and going beyond your horizons. When you do this, you unlock more capacity than you ever thought possible to take the next giant step forward and transport yourself into a universe tailor-made by you. Challenging yourself can help you amplify your greatest potential, reach peak performance and experience more positive and energising feelings of elation and empowerment.

Your comfort zone is a place that is familiar to you; essentially, it is your routine. That is where you feel most relaxed and safe. There is very little stress in the comfort zone. Routine sets you up with a foundational support structure, and life becomes very easy. In routine you can have some rest, be a bit productive and take a break. Staying in your comfort zone for extended periods of time is like being on holiday, but only in one place, with the same food and the same people. As pleasurable as routine might feel, it can quickly lose its vibrancy.

Treat your comfort zone like a home base and venture out from it into the world to grow and evolve.

We all live within comfort zones in different areas of our lives. What does your comfort zone look like? Are you:

» holding back from starting a new business?
» staying in a relationship that is just okay, when in your heart you know you want out?
» putting food in your body that you know doesn't improve your health?
» staying in your job and not pushing for a promotion or a new challenge?
» living in a cluttered environment?
» surrounding yourself with people who don't hold you to your highest potential?

Stepping out of your comfort zone from time to time can lead to great personal achievement and growth. Who doesn't want that? The reason is simple – if you stay inside your comfort zone all the time, nothing changes. You don't grow. You're not challenged. You don't get to find out what you're made of. Instead, you're comfortable. Life's easy. The unique recipe for your comfort zone is determined by your long list of dreams and desires that you haven't achieved. If your list is long, chances are you need to step outside of your comfort zone more often and start ticking things off your list.

Going outside your comfort zone will work that muscle of reaching a little further and will optimise your life, bringing increased:

GROWTH – Stepping outside of the familiar will lead to new growth and development. Even if you make a mistake, you are expanding your knowledge, life skills and personal awareness as well as expanding your comfort zone.

CREATIVITY – When you seek new experiences, learn new skills and open new doors, you will become inspired and motivated.

ADAPTABILITY – You really don't know what potential you have and what you are made of until you step outside of the familiar.

PRODUCTIVITY – Pushing your personal boundaries can help you to get more done. It can make you more ambitious and give you the drive to learn new things: to do more, to be more.

When you want to make changes and move out of your comfort zone, you can start to ask questions like:

- » What is the worst-case scenario that might happen?
- » How *likely* is this to happen?
- » Does this worst-case scenario really need to hold me back from making this change?

Once you have asked these questions, you can begin challenging yourself to step outside your comfort zone and stretch your capabilities in a number of areas of your life, such as:

1. **HEALTH** – What does it look like to step out of your comfort zone for better health? Where can you upgrade your health? Can you improve your diet? Can you move your body more? Can you improve the quality of your sleep? Can you improve the time you allocate to self-care?

2. **CAREER** – What does your dream job look like? Do you have a mentor? How are you moving forward and upgrading your skills? Is there a business you would like to begin? Ask yourself, is this my comfort zone or my launch pad? What would it look and feel like to step out of your comfort zone with your career?

3. **TRAVEL** – What cities would you love to visit? What cultures would you like to experience? How often would you like to travel? What themed holidays would you like to take – a health retreat? A cooking tour? A bike-riding tour? A hiking trail? What would it look and feel like to step out of your comfort zone through travel?

4. **RELATIONSHIPS** – What would it take to have deep, meaningful connections with those closest to you? Where do you need to move out of your comfort zone to be the best version of yourself in your relationships? Are you present and focused when you are with the most important people in your life? Are you a fun and inspiring influence on your family? What would it look and feel like to step out of your comfort zone in your relationships?

5. **FRIENDSHIPS** – How can you extend your friendship circle? How can you be a positive and inspiring influence on your friends? Do you show up being an honest, authentic, kind, caring version of yourself? Where can you let go of your judgement of the important people in

your life? What would it look and feel like to step out of your comfort zone with your friendships?

6. **HOBBIES** – What hobbies have you previously enjoyed? How can you accommodate these in your life? What is a new hobby that you have often thought about but never tried? Where are you creative? How can you be *more* creative? What would it look and feel like to step out of your comfort zone with your hobbies?

7. **FINANCES** – Who is your financial mentor? Are you constantly upgrading your knowledge of your financial position? Where can you move out of your comfort zone with your finances? What would it look and feel like to step out of your comfort zone with your finances?

8. **ENVIRONMENT** – How can you upgrade your work and home environment to be clutter free? Is your wardrobe organised and easy to use? Is your car clean? What would it look and feel like to step out of your comfort zone with your environment?

Most successful people are in the constant habit of stepping out of their comfort zone in things both big and small, continually exercising the habit and reinforcing their confidence to live a greater life. Your dreams won't come to you – you have to leave your comfort zone and chase them down.

Emerging from your comfort zone is something you can learn step by step. The more you practise, the easier it will be. Set yourself small, manageable goals, like walking a different path to work, trying a salsa dancing class or going out and ordering a new cuisine, and reap the benefits that stepping out of your comfort zone has to offer.

All the concepts about stepping out of your comfort zone mean nothing until you decide that your essential purpose, vision and goals are more important than your self-imposed limitations.

———

ROBERT WHITE

15

Adversity

Adversity is like
a strong wind.
It tears from us
all but the things
that cannot be torn,
so that we see
ourselves as
we really are.

———

ARTHUR GOLDEN

EMBRACE FAILURE

Adversity is inevitable, but difficulties or misfortunes don't have to keep you from achieving your goals and finding the happiness you seek in business and in life. It's how you overcome these adversities that can make all the difference. Overcoming adversity can help us expand our internal barriers and build our emotional muscle of resilience, and grow in ways that ultimately make us wiser and our lives more fulfilling.

When looking back at your life, you will regret the chances and opportunities you didn't take more than those you did. We all have a different definition of failure, simply because we all have different benchmarks, values and belief systems. A failure to one person might simply be a great learning experience for someone else. Many of us are afraid of failing, at least some of the time. But fear of failure is when you allow that fear to stop you doing things that can move you forward towards achieving your goals.

The wonderful thing about failure is that it's entirely up to you to decide how you look at it. You can choose to see failure as the end of the world, or you can look at failure as a valuable learning experience, which it often is.

It is easy to find examples of successful people who have experienced failure, such as:

» Richard Branson, owner of the Virgin empire, is a high-school dropout.
» Warren Buffett, one of the world's richest and most successful businessmen, was rejected by Harvard Business School.
» Michael Jordan is considered one of the best basketball players of all time; however, he was cut from his high-school basketball team.

Think of the opportunities you'll miss if you let your failures stop you. If you try and don't succeed, at least you have learned. You only fail by not trying.

The key to mastering failure and adversity is to find value and meaning in setbacks, and to use adversity as a tool to make us more resilient and wise throughout life. Numerous studies have supported the conclusion that adversity toughens us, deepens our understanding of life and ourselves, and, in the end, leaves us with hard-earned wisdom – the bittersweet fruit of adversity. It is a natural part of the road to success. When it's time to move forward, acknowledge what you have gained from the challenges you have overcome. Don't allow adversity to distract you from your purpose. Think about your goals and how important they are to your life's direction.

EMBRACING ADVERSITIES

1. **LIFE LESSONS** – Whenever you face an adversity, the important thing is how you perceive it. What lesson can be learned? All adversities will test your tolerance and patience. Try to always see the positive you can take from a situation, the life lesson, because whenever you feel powerless, like something is happening to you, you can forget your true inner strength.

2. **PROBLEMS OR POSSIBILITIES?** – Adversities can help you put things in perspective. When you focus on problems you have more problems; when you focus on possibilities, you have more opportunities.

3. **WHAT ARE YOU CONTROLLING?** – When you experience an adversity, it frustrates you because you realise that control is an illusion. Even though it sometimes feels like you have

full control of your life, you actually don't have any ability to control external events. The only thing you can control is your internal condition. Once you understand this, you can start to ask, is this adversity really such a roadblock or is it something you can move past?

4. **LIVE IN THE PRESENT** – When you face an adversity or a setback, you have to step forward, because that is the only way to arrive at where you were before. If you keep procrastinating and ruminating on what's happened, you'll stay stuck in the past. When you step forward, you align yourself in the present moment and the power that is in the now.

5. **PRIORITISE YOUR HEALTH** – When you experience adversity, your health can sometimes take a back seat. This is a time when you need the support of good health more than any other. It is the time you need nourishing food to provide energy, exercise to clear your thoughts and good-quality sleep to ensure you have greater perspective. In times when you experience stress, your health is your most reliable tool to keep you balanced and emotionally present.

6. **CALCULATED RISKS** – Practise taking calculated risks. Risks are everywhere, and anything you do might result in failure. Decide how important the risk is versus the risk of not being successful. You will never succeed unless you try.

7. **GET A MENTOR ON BOARD** – Make a list of people you know who have overcome adversity and setbacks to achieve success in their lives. These are the people to seek out to explore the pros and cons with you.

The more you grow with acceptance, the stronger you become and the more you can face. Perhaps the most important question is, are you a victim of circumstance or are you the architect of your destiny? Adversity can build you up or bring you down. It depends on your lens and your choices that follow the setbacks, trials and unfortunate events that you face.

16

Leadership

What you do has far greater impact than what you say.

STEPHEN COVEY

NEXT-LEVEL LEADERSHIP

You are a leader. We can all raise the bar on our leadership skills. Leading is a mindset, a way of living, and you don't need a title to be a leader. Allow yourself to disrupt mediocrity and tap into your personal power to enhance your influence and legacy. Amplify your unapologetic greatness and step up to develop your leadership style. Awaken yourself to living and working with passion, pride and love to heighten your leadership qualities and maximise your results in life.

Leadership is not confined to the boardroom or to leading a team. Rather, it is the pursuit of being the best version of yourself, of adopting the mindset of personal life mastery and becoming a leader of your own lifestyle. Those who rise up, raise the bar, burst forth and embrace courage have an extraordinary commitment to being a leader in their own life, empowering others and extending their personal life strategies for results.

Whether you are a teacher, a taxi driver, a CEO, an athlete, a full-time mum, a hospitality worker, a business owner, an artist, a politician or a musician, world-class leadership comes from a commitment to developing yourself and being the director of your personal journey. It is your ability to stretch, to shift your motivation to a higher gear, to inspire, to persist, to stay unique and be a student of life.

Next-level leadership requires inner focus. It involves you tuning in with great awareness into the business of You Incorporated. It means taking full control of your actions, upgrading your impact and being the CEO of your own life.

Here are some Essentialists leadership thought-starters to apply to your life, refer back to and practise daily to learn and grow as a leader.

Essential Health – Continually concentrate on, upgrade and invest in physical, emotional and mental wellness so you can be there for your team and inspire them to do the same.

Essential Growth – A great leader never stops learning. Not only does this constantly optimise your management skills, it also demonstrates that learning and development is practised across all levels of the organisation.

Essential Mindset – Growth-mindset leaders don't believe that talent and ability are fixed quantities. They understand that abilities and skills can be nurtured, encouraged and developed through effort, perseverance and examining the learning process.

Essential Focus – Let go of the need to compare and compete with others. There is room for everyone to make a contribution. Run your own race and share in others' success.

Essential Strategy – In simple terms, strategic thinking is having an idea or vision of where you want to be and the steps you need to take to achieve that. Leaders don't let bumps in the road distract them from the bigger picture.

Essential Communication – Leaders need skills in working with others on a one-to-one basis and in a group setting. For this reason, you need a range of styles in your communication toolkit to deal with a wide range of situations.

Essential Integrity – Leading by example is an authentic leadership style that demonstrates the ability to walk the talk. This is an indispensable part of fostering the right mindset in any business or organisation.

Essential Honesty – A transparent culture is the foundation of trust. Trust breeds trust, so managers should give their employees the same trust they wish employees to give in return.

Next-level leadership is a joy ride to jump on, a challenge to set yourself to raise your own bar. Through developing leadership skills you will learn something useful that will improve your life, the way you feel, the way you communicate and the way you interact with others. Being a leader is about developing personal strategies to enhance your life, no matter what your profession or age, so you can live an ever-evolving and ultra-inspiring life.

One of the most
important things for
any leader is to never
let anyone else define
who you are.And
you define who you are.
I never think of myself
as being a woman CEO
of this company.
I think of myself as
a steward of a
great institution.

———

GINNI ROMETTY, CEO OF IBM

Purpose

There's no greater gift than to honour your life's calling. It's why you were born. And how you become most truly alive.

OPRAH WINFREY

ALIGN YOUR ACTIONS

A purpose is a master plan for your life. Knowing your purpose helps you define your goals. It helps you avoid getting distracted in the detail of daily life by keeping your eyes on your macro life targets. It can make life more enjoyable and effortless. Purpose is not something someone else chooses for you, it is something you have to choose for yourself. It emerges from an exploration of what you value most. Your purpose should fill you with passion. It can be simple and safe or bold and daring. Living life on purpose will translate to better wellbeing for you, your family and your world.

Start from where you are now and purposefully commit to moving forward with hope and enthusiasm, knowing you are creating your own rich, meaningful life. Take time to uncover and identify your purpose, and allow it to be expressed each day in your work, play and relationships. When you know your purpose, it becomes easier to focus on what matters most in your life and stay away from distractions.

Purpose sets the context for your life. Without a clearly defined purpose, you are just a mixture of goals and non-goals, and actions and non-actions.

Living on purpose feels alive, clear and authentic. In her groundbreaking book *The How of Happiness: A practical guide to getting the life you want*, positive psychologist Sonja Lyubomirsky wrote that a mere 10 per cent of our happiness can be attributed to differences in extrinsic life circumstances or situations like money, fame and status. Our behaviour – what we do and how we think – has much more impact.

Your purpose is what propels you forward in times of success and happiness, and also in the depths of despair. People who find their purpose tend to live in the flow. They allow things to happen and change their life rather than fight against it.

We each have a micro and macro purpose that we live with every day. Together they form your 'why', something that connects and resonates so deeply at your core, something you feel so strongly in every cell of your body, that once you find it you can't imagine what you ever did before without it.

Your micro purpose is to know your values and then live in alignment with them every day. When you know what you stand for and do what you believe in, your confidence and sense of self-worth will be booming regardless of how tricky your current situation is.

Your macro purpose is something different. It's the big picture. It's your search for meaning. It is your ultimate goal. It's waking up in the morning knowing you're on the right track, regardless of what other people say. It is the essence of what brings richness, excitement and fulfilment to your life. For some, knowing what they were born to do comes easily, while others may never know their true purpose, but they will enjoy gathering the hints along the way.

PURPOSE POWER

Knowing your purpose helps you to:

FUEL YOUR PASSION – Knowing your purpose helps you find your true passion, and that passion becomes an important driver for you to achieve something extraordinary. Your passion will push you to reach your goals.

INCREASE GRATITUDE – When you have a purpose in life, you express it constantly and shape your decisions, thoughts, feelings and actions around that overarching purpose. A person who knows their purpose tends to make a greater impact through their work, which encourages feelings of gratitude towards others.

SUPERCHARGE YOUR CLARITY – People who know their purpose in life are unstoppable. They are laser-focused on living in alignment with their purpose, and they construct their lives around that.

ALIGN YOUR VALUES – If your purpose is your big vision in life, your overarching reason for getting out of bed, your values are the daily tools that you use to stay in alignment with your purpose. Our values are health, finances and family. These guide our decisions every day. When you know your purpose you can commit to your values, which are a vital component of your life. Values are the guideposts that shape your decisions and help define your goals.

LIVE WITH INTEGRITY – People who know their purpose in life know who they are, what they are and why they are. And when you know yourself, it becomes easier to live a life that's true to your core values.

FIND THE FUN FACTOR – Even the dullest thing becomes fun and creative when you are motivated by purpose. You are able to take pleasure in living a purpose-driven life and are better at approaching situations in a creative way.

Here are some questions to help you get started in finding your purpose:

> » Why are you reading this now?
> » When do you feel most happy?
> » What are you doing today that will help you be better tomorrow?
> » What are your passions?
> » What are you good at?
> » What makes you stand out from the crowd?
> » What are your non-negotiables in life?
> » What do you believe in?

When you have answers to these questions you can translate those words into a powerful statement that represents what is most important and inspiring to you.

5 HABITS FOR ACCESSING YOUR MICRO AND MACRO PURPOSE

1. **PRESENT-MOMENT LIVING** – When you focus on what you are doing right now, in the present moment, you are aware of the part of the world that you can actually change.

2. **ONE THING** – When you remain focused on one task at a time, you not only do a much better job, you can also find a sense of joy in successfully completing your task.

3. **CHANGE TODAY** – Don't wait until next week to live life more aligned with your micro and macro purpose. Make small changes today. Every day matters.

4. **SERVICE** – Part of your purpose could be to serve others, because it is in service that you will find the greatest inspiration and fulfilment, and it will allow you to live in a place of kindness and connection.

5. **PRACTICE MAKES PURPOSE** – The difference between a life of fulfilment and one of discontentment ultimately comes down to your intention to practise growth every day, to become a version of yourself living in alignment with your true purpose.

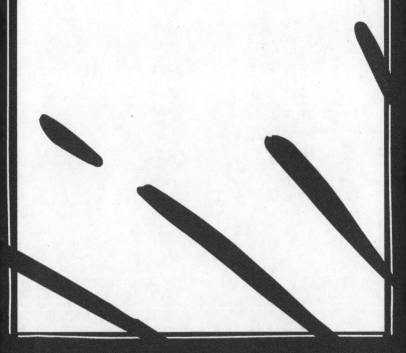

18

Bucket list

Stop dreaming about your bucket list and start living it.

ANNETTE WHITE

UPGRADE YOUR BUCKET LIST

Let your imagination soar, get ultra-inspired and ignite the fire in your belly again by upgrading your bucket list. If you don't have a dream, how can your dream come true? As someone once wisely said, 'Your imagination is the preview to life's coming attractions.' Life is an incredible ride to strap in for. There are no rules: this is your wild journey, determined by the choices you make. Using your bucket list you can discover new directions, feed your creativity and shift your life into a higher gear.

As we grow, mature and age, it is awe-inspiring to take a moment to revisit your dreams, imagination and bucket list. In theory, a bucket list is a list of dreams, goals and ideas to challenge yourself with or that you would like to tick off before your time on Earth is over. A bucket list is also a tool for expanding your mind from the here and now, allowing it to soar and be free, and giving you the chance to dream of the greatest life you can possibly imagine. It is never too early or too late to ignite that spark inside you, to tap into your core and connect with what would inspire you to be your greatest self.

A simple bucket list starts with you picking up a pen and paper and writing down the first things that come to mind when you think of what you want to achieve with your life. This might be something you want to learn, somewhere you want to travel or something you would like to try in life. Nothing is too big or too small to be on your bucket list. The difficult part is being true to yourself, being honest with yourself and leaving behind what society, friends and family might think. Embracing your true self, owning with courage that which will make your heart sing, and going with the flow of what you want your own script to look like. You bucket list should comprise items that you deem important and, most significantly, emotionally fulfilling.

Before you start fine-tuning your list, get in touch with your core set of values, get in a quiet and creative space and give yourself permission to dream. Start anew, or refine your old bucket list, but try to prioritise the importance of experiencing things over owning things.

QUESTIONS TO UPGRADE YOUR BUCKET LIST

- » Who would you like to meet?
- » What skills would you like to acquire?
- » What shows or performances would you like to see?
- » What interests you today?
- » What work would make you rich with fulfilment?
- » What travel adventures do you want to experience?
- » What business would you like to work in?
- » What would you do during a staycation?
- » What makes you smile the most?
- » What challenge would most boost your confidence?
- » What made you giddy with excitement when you were a child? What might help you rediscover that feeling?
- » What critical change can you make to your health today that will make your future self smile?
- » What hobby do you want to dive into?
- » What would you do if you knew you could not fail?
- » What can you let go of that is holding you back?
- » What does success mean to you?

Once you have answered these questions, create a wonderful list and choose three that you can commit to starting or achieving in the next year. Then ask yourself, what can you start this *month*? A bucket list is a wonderful playground in which to spark action. You can also return to the list and start (or complete!) one of the activities listed whenever you need to ignite your life with a burst of inspiration.

Successful people regularly ask themselves great questions. Unlock your mighty mission, your powerful potential, your legacy and your inspiration by asking yourself questions. Allow yourself to dream, to seek and to discover what hints of opportunity are right in front of you.

SOME IDEAS FOR YOUR BUCKET LIST

Become a mentor, learn a new recipe, scuba dive, volunteer, visit the home of your ancestors, sit in the stands of a world-class sporting event, see the northern lights, sketch out your novel idea, grow a herb garden, regain your core strength, go on safari, learn to surf, start a podcast, get a tattoo, run a marathon or Color Run, get married, learn a language, create passive income, ride in a hot air balloon, try CrossFit, explore your gut health, master your sleep, hike the Appalachian Trail in the United States, learn archery, create your ultimate music playlist, learn to read music, solve the Rubik's cube, learn to juggle, dine in your city's or country's top-rated restaurant, attend an Olympic games, stop procrastinating, become an early riser, let go of the past, become a PhD, invest in your financial education, hike the Camino de Santiago trail in Europe, prepare your Will, research your family tree, go on a romantic picnic, live near the ocean, go on a yoga retreat, master mindfulness, embrace meditation, learn forgiveness, develop the art of kindness, develop a mindset of fun, become a tour guide, eat escargot, be a part of a flash mob, ride a motorised scooter or Segway, try geocaching, kiss in the rain, go camping, make five new friends, sit on the board of a company or charity, swim under a waterfall, send a message in a bottle.

These dreams, goals and thoughts give you something to aim for. The list will give you seeds to get curious about and play with, bring hope and anticipation, allow for a plan to form, and make your life feel more alive and optimistic. A bucket list allows you to cultivate courage and go forth with a mindset of excitement.

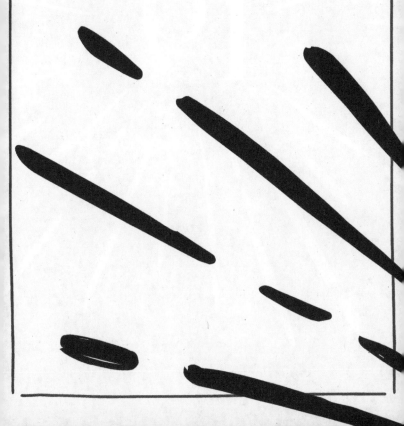

Mentors

A mentor is someone who allows you to see the hope inside yourself.

OPRAH WINFREY

MENTOR OTHERS TO SUCCESS

One of the ways to make success a constant in your life is to help others succeed in their goals. In your own life you have been aided and guided by all kinds of people – colleagues, teachers, friends, family, grandparents, parents and others. Many people have helped you on your way without even realising their impact, by being there for you to ask questions, or showing you a skill you wanted to learn. Sometimes even just spending time with a person is enough to learn from them, as they can be a 'mentor in action' with particular skills you would like to develop more of, like gratitude, kindness, calmness or patience.

Mentoring is a way of helping others as well as helping yourself. Every person you mentor, you can also learn from. You may be able to help someone with a problem similar to one you have faced before. It may be a friend starting a new business, a colleague wanting career advancement, someone going through a major illness or a friend who wants to write a book. As a mentor you are able to shine a light on your mentee's talents and strengths so they can unleash a stronger, more focused version of themselves.

Part of the privilege of mentoring is being able to share your successes and also your learnings, so your mentee can avoid making the same mistakes and fast-track their own personal performance. You can become completely invested in the process and, as a result, their success is also your success. It is a connected process that helps your mentee feel unstoppable, understood, mindful and bulletproof.

If you want to learn something new or dive deeper into a topic, taking on new mentees is a great way to force yourself to make that shift and upgrade on your own knowledge and skills. You may find that you are mentoring on life skills or your professional expertise; no matter what the dimension is, be willing to give your time and attention to help someone else learn the things you already know. A mentee, coming at a problem from a different angle, can also help you to see a new perspective on the issue. Be confident when sharing your perspective and help your mentee think differently. Mentors are not saints, nor do they know everything. But it feels good to nurture talent or help someone when they really need it.

LEARN FROM A MENTOR

As well as mentoring others, you need to think about your own needs. Having the guidance, encouragement and support of a trusted and experienced mentor can ultimately lead to improved performance and help you amplify your talents and maximise your opportunities.

We enlist a new mentor every year in an area into which we want to dive deeper. We are always striving to populate our professional and personal lives with people at a higher level than we are. Given we think like and perform like the people that we surround ourselves with, we choose to always have mentors around us who are inspirational, successful, exceptional experts and passionate human beings. By having a mentor, we raise the bar on our standards in terms of our family rituals, our beliefs, our business, the food we eat, the way we move our bodies, the conversations we have and the accountability we hold.

If you want to minimise your stress, maximise your happiness and reach mastery in your life skills, then you can really benefit from having mentors to guide you along the path to world-class standards. Your mentor can help you gain self-awareness and respect, and build your strengths. When you look at the direction you want to travel in your life, give yourself the opportunity to enlist someone who will hold you accountable and encourage you. A mentor will help you optimise and upgrade your game.

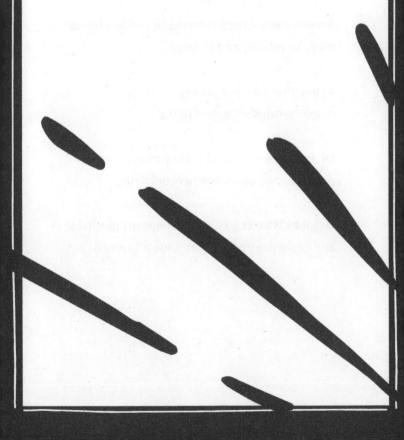

SOME OF OUR MENTORS

Alain de Botton – For bridging the gap from philosophical thinking to a practical way of living.

Oprah Winfrey – For constantly looking at what is unique in each individual and sharing it with the world.

Brené Brown – For her research and teachings on vulnerability and courage.

Robin Sharma – For his supercharged, mastery-mindset way of living.

Dr James Rouse – For his deep insights on peak performance and wholehearted living.

Dr Libby Weaver – For her extensive knowledge and expertise on food, life and optimum living.

Dr Wayne Dyer – For sharing his insights on living life in a deeper state of connection and happiness.

Louise Hay – For sharing her accessible, self-healing, practical insights through books and meditations.

Tim Ferriss – For bringing to the world the insights of inspirational role models with his interviews.

His Holiness the 14th Dalai Lama – For giving over his life to sharing the teachings of Buddhism and living a life of compassion.

Most people love to be asked to guide and give advice to others; it makes them feel valued, expert and important. Take action and make contact with your potential mentors. If you are not in the same country as they are, then watch them from afar and keep learning from them. Have them as a source of inspiration in your life. When you are faced with a decision and you are not sure what to do, ask yourself, 'What would my role model do here?' Then take action!

20

Body language

I speak two
languages:
Body and
English.

MAE WEST

THE POWER OF
BODY LANGUAGE

The amount of confidence you express can have a direct impact on your success. To become an outstanding communicator, understanding body language can go a long way towards helping you deliver exceptional clarity, confidence, trust and warmth when you communicate with others. Body language is the unspoken element of communication that can reveal your true feelings and emotions. Understanding the non-verbal cues from body language is a powerful tool that can help you connect more deeply with others, more clearly express what you mean and build exceptional, quality relationships.

When you interact with others, you continuously give verbal and non-verbal messages. All of your non-verbal behaviours – the gestures you make, the way you sit, how close to someone you stand and how much eye contact you make, et cetera – send a strong message. These messages don't stop when you finish speaking, either. When you are silent you are still communicating non-verbally. The way you listen, look, move and react tells the person who is talking whether you are engaged in the conversation or not.

When we talk about body language we look at the subtle cues we send and receive to each other through movements or postures of the body. According to experts, these non-verbal signals make up a major part of our daily communication. When your non-verbal signals match up with the words you're saying, they increase trust, clarity and rapport. From your facial expressions to your body movements, the things you don't say can still convey volumes of information. When you are able to read these signs in other people, you can use it to your advantage to help you understand the complete message of what someone is saying to you and enhance your awareness of people's reactions to what you say and do.

Your body language communicates not only who you are to others, it also relays messages back to you, impacting how you feel in different situations. When you stand in a 'power pose', like a superhero – with your legs hip-width apart, shoulders back and chest strong, and your arms comfortably by your sides – it will not only make you appear confident to others, but mentally, emotionally, and physically, you will begin to feel more confident. Upgrading your communication skills is acknowledging that often body language matters more than the words you say.

It has been suggested that body language may account for between 50 to 70 per cent of all communication. Dr Amy Cuddy, body language expert, social psychologist and award-winning Harvard University lecturer, has proposed that when you privately stand in power poses for a couple of minutes before going into a stressful situation, there will be changes in your body chemistry that make you feel more confident and in command. Cuddy says, 'When an individual has power, they take up more space. If you adopt these postures you are more likely to feel confident and see the world in a way that is filled with opportunities rather than challenges. If someone is seen as confident then they are also seen as competent.'

You can change your body language, but, like all new habits, it takes time and commitment to do so. Take a couple of these body language tips and work on them every day for the next month. Over this time you'll develop more awareness around the habit and it will become something you do automatically. If not, keep at it until it sticks.

10 POWERFUL BODY LANGUAGE TIPS TO INSTANTLY BOOST YOUR CONFIDENCE

1. **PERFECT POSTURE** – Relaxed and upright is a happy medium. When you are sitting, leaning slightly forward indicates that you are listening and engaged.

2. **EYE CONTACT** – Establishing strong eye contact at the beginning of a conversation immediately communicates confidence and tells the other person that that you are present and ready.

3. **FORGET THE FIDDLING** – Instead of fiddling mindlessly, use hand gestures on purpose to reinforce your point.

4. **HANDS AWAY** – Keep your hands away from your face, as they can communicate negative gestures.

5. **STAND STRONG** – Be graceful, composed and expansive. Take up space: the more space you take up, the more confident you appear to others.

6. **POWER POSES** – Take a couple of minutes to stand in a superhero pose before a meeting or presentation to allow your hormones to support your inner power.

7. **DRESS FOR CONFIDENCE** – When you dress appropriately for the situation, know your audience, reflect your own unique style and understand the impact of colour, you can boost your confidence.

8. **PRACTISE SMILING** – According to several studies, smiling can trick your brain into feeling happy, even when you feel uneasy or sad.

9. **AVOID CROSSING YOUR ARMS AND LEGS** – This is a sign of closing off and being uninterested.

10. **STRONG HANDSHAKE** – A firm, strong handshake transmits your underlying confidence in yourself and your abilities.

And finally

All that remains is for us to wish you good health and good luck in your own search for your spark. The skills and strategies you have discovered will help you ignite the successful and empowered life you deserve.

Shannah and Lyndall – *The Essentialists*

ABOUT THE ESSENTIALISTS
OUR MISSION

The Essentialists work to engage, educate and empower individuals, teams and organisations with essential life and wellness skills.

The Essentialists help people take control of their health, wellbeing and ultimately their happiness by committing to what is essential in both their personal and professional lives, through the mastery of fundamental life and wellness skills. Their commitment is to equip people with the tools they need to make the best, wisest and most authentic investment of their time and energy in their one and only precious life.

The Essentialists' way isn't about doing more, it's about doing what's right for you, wherever you are in life's journey. This clarity allows for far more effective work and self-care practices that ultimately lead to breakthroughs in work and life. Better leadership, human connections, self-care, gratitude, empathy and joy in the everyday. The results of The Essentialists' programs are testimony to this.

SMALL CHANGES –
BIG IMPACT

Our mission is to teach the art of simplicity using vital life and wellness skills for empowered living.

We provide the pathways for transformational change.

Everything we produce exists to simply inspire and educate people on how to become the best versions of themselves and ignite their potential.

WHO ARE THE ESSENTIALISTS?

Shannah Kennedy and Lyndall Mitchell
Educators of life and wellness skills

Shannah and Lyndall are acknowledged as Australia's leaders in life and wellness education. They combine more than three decades of teaching, presenting and executive coaching experience across public and corporate sectors globally. Their books, *Chaos to Calm: Take control with confidence*, *Shine: 20 secrets to a happy life* and *Restore: 20 self-care rituals to reclaim your energy*, have helped many people create extraordinary lives.

Together, Shannah and Lyndall offer a wealth of experience, complementary expertise and strategies to maximise impact for their clients. As working mothers juggling family with thriving businesses and a non-negotiable stance on the importance of their own health and wellbeing, their commitment to basic fundamental life skills ensures they stay on track and are constantly evolving to be their best.

For speaking opportunities, inquire at:
info@theessentialists.com.au

Stay inspired, stay connected. Join our global online community for regular, bite-sized life and wellness skills:
theessentialists.com.au
🄾 **theessentialistshub**

ACKNOWLEDGEMENTS

We express our deep appreciation to the entire team at Penguin Random House Australia, who support and believe in our passion to educate the world with essential life and wellness skills.

To our readers and clients who constantly fuel our fire and show gratitude for this incredibly important educational and inspirational work – you keep us fully committed to doing what is essential for us to thrive and live our best lives.